Resist *the* Devil

The Temptations of Christ and Our Temptations

TOM KINGERY

WESTBOW
PRESS®
A DIVISION OF THOMAS NELSON
& ZONDERVAN

WestBow Press books may be ordered through booksellers or by contacting:

WestBow Press
A Division of Thomas Nelson & Zondervan
1663 Liberty Drive
Bloomington, IN 47403
www.westbowpress.com
844-714-3454

ISBN: 978-1-6642-9708-1 (sc)
ISBN: 978-1-6642-9709-8 (e)

Library of Congress Control Number: 2023906488

Print information available on the last page.

WestBow Press rev. date: 04/12/2023

INTRODUCTION

Jesus, full of the Holy Spirit,
returned from the Jordan
and was led by the Spirit in the wilderness,
where for forty days he was tempted by the devil.
—LUKE 4:1–2A

Jesus had just been baptized. He went from the abundant, flowing waters of the Jordan River to the dry, waterless, barren wilderness. The lack of shade left Him exposed to the hot Middle Eastern sun. He was parched. He would have been dehydrated without water to drink. The effects of dehydration can include hallucinations, organ failure, lightheadedness, and fatigue, to name a few. He must have had water now and then—the Bible doesn't say—in order to last forty days. But it was then that He began to be tempted.

I think of Psalm 63:1, where it says, "O God, you are my God, I seek you, my soul thirsts for you; my flesh faints for you, as in a dry and weary land where there is no water."

The Exodus story of the people of faith includes forty years in "the wilderness." "The Lord's anger was kindled against Israel, and he made them wander in the wilderness for forty years ..." (Numbers 32:13a) There was one time when they came to a place where there was no water, and the people complained. But God miraculously provided water for them (Exodus 17:6).

Some scholars speak about "the wilderness" as a setting where people are being prepared. It is where a person can learn a total dependence on God. It is where we have to face ourselves at our "weakest" or in our most desperate needs. In a way, we can discover what we are made of … our fortitude or our ability to persevere. We may not realize it until we are coming out of the wilderness, but God has a purpose for us even when life seems barren. I have known many people who have questioned whether or not God was with them. They felt empty and uninspired. Some have kept going, believing they would feel God's divine presence again … soon. Some have carried on in a search mode, looking for "something" that might touch their hearts again. Some have given up on God or themselves. Some had gotten angry and felt "abandoned." Some just get depressed and feel rejected.

Maybe "the wilderness" is relevant. Maybe even necessary. It can be a time of growth or of sorting, where we sort things out and sometimes change course or cut ourselves off from some of the things that were hindering us from going forward. Personally, I have always wanted to move "forward," whatever that might mean. When you're thirsty, you look for water.

As always, shifting metaphors is almost too easy. *The ocean* is also a "wilderness." It may be teeming with life beneath the surface, but don't drink the water. Part of the human problem that often arises is that sometimes it can feel like we are aimlessly adrift at sea. It's similar to "wandering" in "the wilderness," where there might be no paths. We are moved by currents of which we might not even be aware. And we will want to drink the water even though we know it's not good for us. We can feel anchorless as we drift. And with nothing to really hold us in place, we will be very easily tempted to think that anything that seems to feel good is all right. Any idea might work. It's like the condition of the Israelites during the period of the Judges. In Judges 17:6, the human condition is epitomized: "All the people did what was right in their own eyes."

Temptations come all too easily when we have no sense of direction, or when we have no sense of purpose, or when we feel empty as if God is absent in our lives.

There's the reason for this book. I want us to do an examination of temptation. In the Letter of James, we are told, "One is tempted by one's own desire, being lured and enticed by it; then, when that desire has conceived, it gives birth to sin, and then sin, when it is fully grown, gives birth to death" (James 1:14–15).

"Occasions for stumbling are bound to come, but woe to anyone by whom they come" (Luke 17:1). In the English Standard Version, instead of "stumbling," they use the word "temptation." Temptations are out there and are bound to meet us in our journeys. We need to resist them!

In the "wilderness," Jesus was confronted by three very particular temptations. I intend to examine them and then study in depth His response to them. This sort of process can guide us when we are tempted. But first, let's acknowledge that we do not have the fortitude that Jesus had. He is God incarnate, all powerful, and all knowing. We are human, fallen and much, much weaker. But I believe when we know where temptations are coming from, and we learn how to face them, we can resist them and overcome them … with Christ's help!

So journey with me as we explore the idea of resisting the devil.

"Resist the devil, and he will flee from you" (James 4:7).

Scriptures

To discover more about what the Bible says about temptation and testing, here are some scripture passages that will help to inspire us:

Deuteronomy 8:2 – Remember the long way that the Lord your God led you these forty years in the wilderness in order to humble you, testing you to know what was in your heart, whether or not you would keep his commandments.

Psalm 66:10 – For you, O God, have tested us; you have tried us as silver is tried.

Matthew 6:13 – Do not bring us to the time of trial, but rescue us from the evil one. (**And lead us not into temptation, but deliver us from evil. KJV**)

Matthew 22:18 – "Why are you putting me to the test, you hypocrites?"

Mark 8:11 – The Pharisees came and began to argue with him, asking for a sign from heaven, to test him.

Luke 22:40 – "Pray that you may not come into the time of trial."

John 8:6 – They said this to test him, so they might have some charge to bring against him.

1 Corinthians 10:13 – No testing has overtaken you that is not common to everyone. God is faithful, and he will not let you be tested beyond your strength, but with the testing he will also provide the way out so that you may be able to endure it.

Galatians 6:1 – My friends, if anyone is detected in a transgression, you who have received the Spirit should restore such a one in a spirit of gentleness. Take care that you yourselves are not tempted.

1 Timothy 6-9 – But those who want to be rich fall into temptations and are trapped by many senseless and harmful desires that plunge people into ruin and destruction.

1 Thessalonians 3:5 – I was afraid that the tempter had tempted you and that our labor had been in vain.

Hebrews 4:15 – We do not have a high priest who is unable to sympathize with our weakness, but we have one who in every respect has been tested as we are, yet without sin.

James 1:12 – Blessed is anyone who endures temptation. Such one has endured the test and will receive the crown of life that the Lord has promised to those who love him.

James 4:1–4 – Those conflicts and disputes among you, where do they come from? Do they not come from your cravings that are at war within you? You want something and do not have it; so you commit murder. And you covet something and cannot obtain it, so you engage in disputes and conflicts. You do not have because you do not ask. You ask and do not receive, because you ask wrongly, in order to spend what you get on your pleasures. Adulterers! Do you not know that friendship with the world is enmity with God? Therefore whoever wishes to be a friend of the world becomes an enemy of God.

1 Peter 4:12 – Beloved, do not be surprised at the fiery ordeal that is taking place among you to test you, as though something strange were happening to you.

What to Do

> Don't fear the wilderness.
> Expect to be tempted. But also expect to grow.
> Realize that, by faith, you can endure temptation.
> Try to remember if you have ever been in a wilderness of some kind. What was happening?
> Think about *why* God might lead you into a wilderness-time in your life.
> Think about what you might have "resisted," for whatever reason, in your past. What are you resisting today? What does it mean to "resist" something or someone?

A Prayer

Almighty God, You lead us through the darkness toward a perfect light. Whenever I am challenged by the promise of something I don't need, give me direction. If I have wanted anything the possession of which would not give You glory, change my thoughts to gratitude for what I have already. Let me be content in such a way that I am never tempted by "more." And help me to count my blessings 'til I see fulfillment in my heart because I believe in Jesus Christ, my Lord and my all. In His great name, I pray. Amen.

A Poem

My Heart Becomes a Wilderness

My heart becomes a wilderness
When I think about my sin
I'm in an empty, hollow place
Where sleep is cruel and dreams are thin

My mind just wanders aimlessly
I just can't find my way.
Something needs to pilot me
My soul has lost its way

It hurts me when I take a breath
In this barren field of pain
I believe that even Death
Would somehow go insane.

But somewhere deep inside—a light
Is shining in this nasty night.

CHAPTER ONE

BREAD

He ate nothing at all during those days,
and when they were over, he was famished.
The devil said to him,
"If you are the Son of God,
command this stone to become a loaf of bread."
—LUKE 4:2B–3

In the Gospel of John, after Jesus fed five thousand people with "five barley loaves and two fish" (John 6:9), He withdrew to be by Himself (John 6:15). Meanwhile, the disciples got into a boat and headed across the Sea of Galilee toward Capernaum. But Jesus was not with them. Instead, He *walked* across the water. And the next day, some of the five thousand came looking for Him. The boat was gone, and they knew that Jesus had not been in it when the disciples took off. But they still got into the other boats and rowed across to Capernaum, looking for Jesus.

> When they found him on the other side of the sea, they said to him, "Rabbi, when did you come here?" Jesus answered them, "Very truly, I tell you, you are looking for me, not because you saw signs, but because you ate your fill of the loaves. Do not work for the food that

perishes, but for the food that endures for eternal life, which the Son of Man will give you. For it is on him that God the Father has set his seal." Then they said to him, "What must we do to perform the works of God?" Jesus answered them, "This is the work of God, that you believe in him whom he has sent" (John 5:25–29).

Bread

Bread is one of the oldest human-made foods. Flour, water, and usually salt and leaven are mixed together to create a dough, which is kneaded, baked, and served with other foods. Often, in antiquity, bread, especially the hard crust, was used to carry other food to the mouth. And because it was absorbent, bread went well with soups and sauces.

But bread is also a staple food and brings fiber, among other nutrients, to the body. For the poor in many cultures, it is vital and is often one of the few sources of food eaten regularly. It is even possible to live on bread alone, but it is better to have a more complete meal in order to receive all the vitamins and nutrients the body needs.

Even the five thousand were filled enough to carry on for the rest of their day. And I have known people who have eaten nothing but bread for several weeks and survive fairly well. But it is not recommended, and they did lose weight. Bread, sorry to say, is not always "enough." But it does help sustain us.

And it is that sustaining ability that bread often symbolizes in scripture, as in Matthew 6:11, "Give us this day our daily bread."

So Jesus encouraged the followers who caught up to Him near Capernaum to look for more than just physical sustenance. He wanted them to find "the food that endures for eternal life" (John 6:27). And finding this food is *a life-giving* truth. Only their physical hunger had been satisfied. From that experience, they believed Jesus could produce plenty more where that came from. He was suddenly seen as a free meal ticket. But Jesus is so much more. He is the Bread of Life.

And I mentioned that finding "the food that endures to eternal life" is a life-giving truth. Well, there are many life-giving truths to learn, and

I believe that, in this study, we will find a few more. Some of what we learn can be very enriching and nourishing for our spiritual journeys. That's what makes them so life-giving. When we learn them, we can feel more alive, closer to God, and more mature in our faith. They help us grow. And we need to "seek the things that are above, where Christ is …" (Colossians 3:1)

The Bread of Life

These followers needed to discover "the food that endures for eternal life, which the Son of Man will give you" (John 6:27). They wanted this, and maybe they wanted it as much as ordinary bread. So they asked Jesus how it could happen. They needed to believe. "What sign are you going to give us then, so that we may see it and believe you?" (John 6:30) Sign? Hadn't they just seen five thousand people be fed from five barley loaves and two fish? But again, they were so earthly minded and were hungry—for a sign. "What work are you performing?" (John 6:30b)

"'Our ancestors ate the manna in the wilderness; as it is written, "He gave them bread from heaven to eat."' Then Jesus said to them, 'Very truly, I tell you, it was not Moses who gave you the bread from heaven, but it is my Father who gives you the true bread from heaven. For the bread of God is that which comes down from heaven and gives life to the world.' They said to him, 'Sir, give us this bread always'" (John 6:31–34).

The word "always" there reveals a deep longing and a hopeful sincerity to me. They were true seekers. And then Jesus tells them one of the greatest truths in all scripture: "I am the Bread of Life. Whoever comes to me will never be hungry, and whoever believes in me will never be thirsty" (John 6:35). This is a life-giving truth.

So Jesus was teaching His followers that He is the fulfillment of the spiritual hunger of the world. And later on, Jesus told them, "I am the living bread that comes down from heaven. Whoever eats of this bread will live forever; and the bread that I will give for the life of the world is … my flesh" (John 6:51). Whoa! Just imagine the looks of confusion on everyone's faces and the response of repulsion from the Jewish leaders to the very barbaric and utterly pagan notion of eating Jesus's flesh.

And He even goes on to say, "Very truly, I tell you, unless you eat the flesh of the Son of Man and drink his blood, you have no life in you. Those who eat my flesh and drink my blood have eternal life, and I will raise them up on the last day; for my flesh is true food and my blood is true drink. Those who eat my flesh and drink my blood abide in me and I in them" (John 6:53–56).

Many did not understand His words. And many couldn't tolerate them. But we who have shared the ritual of the communion meal hear echoes of Jesus's words from His last supper. As He broke the bread of that Passover meal, it was His body broken for them—"Take, eat …" And when He took the cup; it was His blood poured out for the forgiveness of sin—"Drink of this."

Symbolic language is awkward at times. But we can understand this eating and drinking as a spiritual act of taking Jesus into our lives. Knowing/believing that as we do, we are accepting the new life He gives, the grace He offers, and the love that never ends. Jesus gave Himself to believers who trust in His Word and His love. The crux of the matter is believing in Jesus! John 6:29 states, "This is the work of God, that you believe in him whom he has sent." This is a life-giving truth.

Command This Stone

Jesus was "famished" (Luke 4:2). He needed something to eat. I imagine He was also thirsty and needed some water. The living bread needed earthly bread. And we all know what it's like to be hungry. We may not know the emptiness of forty days of fasting, but we can understand Jesus's need. People who need food usually don't want anything else at the moment. And it's hard to patiently accept moral platitudes when you are famished.

It's hard to do much else when you're hungry. You might even be too weak to work and earn enough to buy a meal. And you're probably a little irritable, like I get. You can easily feel desperate. And when you're hungry, you'll eat anything, even if it's not good for you. And there are many kinds of hunger.

Loneliness is a kind of hunger. So people will seek companionship even with people who are not good for them. Grief and sadness can also be kinds of hunger, so people will seek happiness even in ways that are only temporary.

But what do our longings, our yearnings, our desires, and our various hungers tell us about ourselves? Obviously, there are needs in our lives. But when our most basic needs are met, we can usually be content. Yet something deep within us is rarely satisfied. We don't just want enough; we want to feel good. More than "good," we want to feel important. We want to feel fulfilled in such a way that our cups seem to overflow. And should they do so, we should bring our abundance to others. And behind it all, always in the background, is the need for food to sustain our bodies—the instinct for self-preservation.

Everyone needs food. This is the first thing we should share when we have more than enough. And I believe that in a world where there is so much abundance that we can call some of the stuff we eat "junk food," no one should go hungry. We just need to do a better job of sharing.

During His fasting, hunger had a hold of Jesus. And Satan tried to get a hold of Him too. Nearby, there were probably several smooth stones, about the size of a loaf of bread. Satan saw the likeness and tempted Jesus to "command this stone to become a loaf of bread ..." (Luke 4:3)

Scriptures

To discover more about what the Bible says about bread, here are some scripture passages that will help to inspire us:

Psalm 132:15 – "I will abundantly bless its provisions, I will satisfy the poor with bread."

Matthew 5:6 – "Blessed are those who hunger and thirst for righteousness, for they will be filled."

Matthew 6:11 – "Give us this day our daily bread."

Matthew 6:25 – "Therefore I tell you, do not worry about your life, what you will eat or what you will drink, or your body, what you will wear. Is not life more than food, and the body more than clothing?"

Matthew 7:9 – "Is there anyone among you who, if your child asks for bread, will give a stone?"

Matthew 16:5–12 – When the disciples reached the other side, they had forgotten to bring any bread. Jesus said to them, "Watch out, and beware of the yeast of the Pharisees and Sadducees." They said to one another, "It is because we have no bread." And becoming aware of it, Jesus said, "You of little faith, why are you talking about having no bread? Do you still not perceive? Do you not remember the five loaves for the five thousand, and how many baskets you gathered? Or the seven loaves for the four thousand, and how many baskets you gathered? How could you fail to perceive that I was not speaking about bread? Beware of the yeast of the Pharisees and Sadducees." Then they understood that he had not told them to beware of the yeast of bread, but of the teaching of the Pharisees and Sadducees.

Matthew 26:26 – While they were eating, Jesus took a loaf of bread, and after blessing it he broke it, gave it to the disciples, and said, "Take, eat, this is my body."

John 4:34 – "My food is to do the will of him who sent me and to complete his work."

1 Corinthians 5:8 – Therefore, let us celebrate the festival, not with the old yeast, the yeast of malice and evil, but with the unleavened bread of sincerity and truth.

1 Corinthians 10:17 – Because there is one bread, we who are many are one body, for we all partake of the one bread.

TOM KINGERY

2 Corinthians 9:10 – He who supplies seed to the sower and bread for food will supply and multiply your seed for sowing and increase the harvest of your righteousness.

What to Do

- Think of Jesus as the Bread of Life.
- Trust that God will meet your needs.
- "Strive first for the kingdom of God and his righteousness, and all these things will be given to you as well" (Matthew 6:33).
- Consider: What is "the food that endures for eternal life"? Are you seeking it?
- Hunger and thirst for righteousness.
- Think about a time when you were hungry. Had you fasted? Had you been dieting? Why were you hungry? How did you feel, physically and emotionally? What did you do?
- Consider: What other types of hunger that I might not have named can you think of?
- Be a positive part in the food chain. Help supply bread to the hungry!
- Serve in a soup kitchen when you can.
- Think: What are some life-giving truths for you?

A Prayer

Almighty God, You can make my words be like bread to the hungry. May we all seek the fulfillment that comes by faith. But help us all also have the grace we need to share food with those who have none and drink with those who thirst. Forgive me when I overeat and help me discover my true longings. Help us, in our culture of abundance, to repent for the sin of "junk food" and lead us in hope to build a world where there is no hunger at all. This I pray in Jesus's name. Amen.

A Poem

When Every Thought Seems Hollow

When every thought seems hollow
And the mind's a vacant space …
When lies are hard to swallow,
It's like nothing leaves a trace.
The paths we want to follow
Disappeared or were erased;
And all we do is wallow
In the mysteries we face
It's then we feel a yearning
For the promises we've known
And hope begins returning
And we don't feel so alone.
Within us all a hunger grows
And it can't just be denied
One dream comes and one dream goes
When other dreams have died.

CHAPTER TWO

NOT BY BREAD ALONE

Remember the long way that the Lord our God has led you
these forty years in the wilderness, in order to humble you,
testing you to know what was in your heart,
whether or not you would keep his commandments.
He humbled you by letting you hunger,
then by feeding you with manna,
with which neither you nor your ancestors were acquainted,
in order to make you understand that
one does not live by bread alone,
but by every word that comes from the mouth of the Lord.

—DEUTERONOMY 8:2–3

How did Jesus face the first temptation in the wilderness? Scripture!

Our God, incarnate in the human form of Jesus, hungered. He was vulnerable. And Satan comes at us often when and where we are vulnerable! "Command this stone to become a loaf of bread" (Luke 4:3). Is that possible? Even for Jesus, who is the Creator that made the stone the way it was, I believe He *could* actually transform the rock. But …

when God created everything, it was all "good" just as it was (Genesis 1:31). "Very good." It shouldn't need to be changed. Not even for the sake of convenience for Jesus's hunger!

I can imagine Jesus thinking about how He made that stone! Maybe it wasn't an easy task. We take Creation for granted so often that we act as if it's just "there." I love the science-fiction idea of how changing something might alter the whole universe. But that's really just an imaginary thing. Or is it? Change is what existence is all about. Faith is about change. We believe in Jesus, most of us, in order to change our destiny from being lost to being saved. God changed the direction of the Israelites after the Exodus and led them into the wilderness to humble them and test them. Their hunger was to help them learn that "one does not live by bread alone, but by every word that comes from the mouth of the Lord" (Deuteronomy 8:3). Another life-giving truth! And He fed them miraculously by giving them manna—helping them know that He could provide.

It was with this truth that Jesus resisted that first temptation. And this truth needs to stand out more powerfully than we usually let it. It is an overarching reality that gives strength and awareness about all things, in every issue we face, in every struggle we endure. We are to live by God's Word—a life-giving truth.

A Lamp to My Feet

I love Psalm 119:105 – "Your word is a lamp to my feet and a light to my path." In a way, that says it all. Another life-giving truth. But for that light to exist in our lives, we need to learn the Word. We need to know it, practice it, and remember it. Light in the darkness or at night in Jesus's day came from fire—an oil lamp or hearth fire, a torch, or bonfire. In order to have light, a small stick would be touched to one fire in order to pass the flame to another source, where it could burn and bring light. In the same way as we often take Creation for granted, we take light for granted—assuming it is just "there" when we want it. Realize, though, that light takes work, energy. It doesn't just "happen." Perhaps Psalm 119:105 was well known in Jesus's time as a reminder that we should appreciate the light of God's Word. And perhaps Deuteronomy 8:3 was even more well known among Jews, recited now and then as a reminder of the importance of knowing the truth. There are many life-giving truths like these that can be like pearls in our store of treasures.

How well do you remember things? I'm like everyone. I went into the back room, and when I got there, I completely forgot why I went. We all do that. I think that sometimes we're just absent-minded. But could it be true that the longer we live, the more we have to remember? And with so much to remember, there is always more to forget. I can remember complete dialogues from my past very easily, but I can't remember the password I set for my computer just one day ago. We joke about these things. The person at the mailbox is confounded because the letter she was supposed to send, she opened it instead.

I can remember my reaction to the first time I saw a rerun on television. I was a kid. I don't remember, oddly enough, what show it was, but I remember my reaction to this discovery. It's amazing how the mind works and how it often reconstructs an experience. Sporting events will replay an episode of a game, sometimes several times and in slow motion, in order to discover exactly what happened. Did the runner touch the base in time? Where did the tackle actually occur? How did she do that flip? The camera usually catches what our eyes might not. We trust those replays. We rely on what we're shown. And we need to replay the truths of God's Word often in our minds. Remembering what God or the prophets or Jesus said can be a great source of strength when we need to resist temptations. But sometimes we can even be tempted by our memories.

Some memories come back to haunt us. They tempt us to hold on to grudges or to think better of ourselves than we should. The compliment of one person usually outweighs the criticism of another. But that criticism sure gnaws away at us. The enticement of a destination draws us like a strong gravitational force. But some of that is just about choices. But that's what temptations are all about: choices. I joked the other day about the person who went to worship on a foul rainy day. That afternoon his friend asked him, "When you started out your day, what made you decide to go to church in this weather?" And the man said, "I didn't make the decision this morning, I made it decades ago!"

It's funny to know that Sunday comes every week, and we can decide on Monday that we'll be in worship when it comes. Of course, we can all be "fair-weather" Christians at times. Sometimes we might actually stay home because we don't feel well, and we don't want to make others sick.

Jesus resisted the temptation to feed Himself by knowing what His real need was. It is God's Word that feeds us best. When we focus on the Word of the kingdom, often everything else we might be anxious about will fall into place. "Strive first for the kingdom of God and his righteousness, and all these things will be given to you as well" (Matthew 6:33). Another life-giving truth. Haven't I already said that somewhere before? But we can choose our focus! Remember your choices! Remember the Word!

This temptation was to be self-centered. It was about His hunger, His need, His weakness. Satan threw all that in His face. I don't want to minimize the desperation of hunger, and I've already said that when you're hungry, it's hard not to want to do something about it. But it *can* be wrong to put up a mirror before someone that reveals their need or their weakness.

Jesus knew something more important than His physical hunger. He knew about His eternal kingdom. He remembered what was truly relevant. Can we do that? Can we deny ourselves for the sake of God's kingdom? One lesson we can gain from this temptation of Christ is that there is something more to life than just living. We might perpetuate our existence with food, but to truly live includes God—that idea is life-giving.

So how do we deny our personal needs, wants, and wishes? First, be focused beyond yourself. When we focus our attention on the needs of others or of the world, we can get out of ourselves. I like the autobiography of Gale Sayers, a famous football running back. The title is *I Am Third*. He says, "God is first, others are second, and I am third." When we can get these priorities right in our lives, things work better.

Second, let go of pride. We need to think of others as more important than ourselves (Philippians 2:3b). We get caught up in having a good reputation, a great house, a wonderful car, a big salary, etc. But when we let go of these desires/temptations, we become truer to our purpose in God's estimation for us.

TOM KINGERY

Third, deny the idea of being honored for your achievements. Such is the way of the world. Life is not a competition. We are all part of the team of humanity. It may be nice to receive accolades, but we ought to bless others with what blesses us.

Fourth, relinquish any sense of how you want to live by your own rules. We rebel against any authority that does not agree with the way we think things should be. We don't like accountability and we don't want to be judged by any standards other than our own.

So be accountable to God. Put your will, your life under God's authority. Let go of the idea that you need to accomplish great things in order to be happy. Sure, our accomplishments can please us, but they are not an end in themselves. You don't need to change reality. We don't need to change stones into bread. We need the Bread of Life. We need to remember that we "do not live by bread alone, but by every word that comes from the mouth of God!"

Scriptures

To discover more about what the Bible says about God's Word, here are some scripture passages that will help to inspire us:

2 Timothy 3:16–17 – All scripture is inspired by God and is useful for teaching, for reproof, for correction, and for training in righteousness, so that everyone who belongs to God may be proficient, equipped for every good work.

Psalm 119:9 – How can young people keep their way pure? By guarding it according to your word.

Psalm 119:114 – You are my hiding place and my shield; I hope in your word.

Isaiah 40:8 – The grass withers, the flower fades; but the word of our God will stand forever.

Matthew 7:24 – "Everyone who hears these words of mine and acts on them will be like a wise man who built his house on rock …"

Matthew 24:35 – "Heaven and earth will pass away, but my words will not pass away."

Luke 11:28 – "Blessed rather are those who hear the word of God and obey it."

John 1:1 – In the beginning was the Word, and the Word was with God. and the Word was God.

John 1:14 – And the Word became flesh and lived among us, and we have seen his glory, the glory as of a father's only son, full of grace and truth.

John 15:7 – "If you abide in me, and my words abide in you, ask for whatever you wish, and it will be done for you."

John 17:17 – "Sanctify them in the truth; your word is truth."

Romans 15:4 – Whatever was written in former days was written for our instruction, so that by steadfastness and by the encouragement of the scriptures we might have hope.

Ephesians 5:17 – Take the helmet of salvation, and the sword of the Spirit, which is the word of God.

Philippians 2:14–16a – Do all things without murmuring and arguing, so that you may be blameless and innocent; children of God without blemish in the midst of a crooked and perverse generation, in which you shine like stars in the world. It is by your holding fast to the word of life that I can boast on the day of Christ.

Colossians 3:16 – Let the word of Christ dwell in you richly; teach and admonish one another in all wisdom; and with gratitude in your hearts sing psalms hymns, and spiritual songs to God.

Hebrews 4:12 – Indeed, the word of God is living and active, sharper than any two-edged sword, piercing until it divides soul from spirit, joints from marrow; it is able to judge the thoughts and intentions of the heart.

1 Peter 2:2 – Like newborn babes, long for the pure, spiritual milk, so that by it you may grow into salvation …

James 1:21 – Therefore rid yourselves of all sordidness and rank growth of wickedness, and welcome with meekness the implanted word that has the power to save your soul.

What to Do

> Put your will and your life under God's authority.
> Know where you might be vulnerable in order to be on guard.
> Realize that change is part of life. What does that mean for you?
> Don't take Creation for granted, nor light, nor scriptures you can remember.
> Consider your priorities. What is most important to you?
> Think about ways life seems to be a competition. How can we rise above this idea?

A Prayer

Almighty God, You call us all to love You with all our hearts and minds and strength and soul. Help us to know that that means putting You first. Give us grace to discern our priorities in the light of Your expectations, not our own. Help us trust Your purposes for us and that we need not stress over worldly needs when we remember that You are in control. And help us remember that You *are* in control. This we ask in Jesus's name. Amen.

A Poem

God's Word Is Fire

God's Word is fire and faith is fuel
We bear the torch and praise His rule
Our purpose is to pass the light
To others who have lost their sight.

The Word's a sword that cuts away
The cause of darkness in each day
Our great task is to wield the blade
'Til peace has come and love has stayed

God's Word is rock, a place to stand
Proclaiming truth to every land
And we are echoing the sound
That faith is like the solid ground

The Word's a shield that guards the soul
Against the lies that take their toll
By tempting us when we are weak
And cannot find the fuel we seek

Our hope is just to keep the fire
Burning in each heart's desire.

CHAPTER THREE

THE BIG "IF"

*Then the devil took him to the holy city
and placed him on the pinnacle of the temple,
saying to him,
"If you are the Son of God,
throw yourself down,
for it is written,
'He will command his angels concerning you,'
and 'On their hands they will bear you up,
so that you will not dash your foot against a stone.'"*

—MATTHEW 4:5–6

There's that stone again! Not to be turned into bread, but seen as an obstacle, a threat, an instant injury. But the temptation here includes self-questioning. The primary outward temptation is to prove yourself. "If you are the Son of God ..." To whom does Jesus need to prove Himself? To the devil? Ha!

I liked being on the track-and-field team in high school. When people hear "track and field," most people tend to think of sprints or distance running, the long jump, or the pole vault. Well, I was the shot-putter and the discus-thrower. Not as big a deal as being the fastest or the most enduring. What I liked was that even though I was competing against others for the best distance, I was also competing against myself. I always wanted to accomplish a personal best because if I did, I still felt like I did well, even if I didn't win against all the other competitors in my field. We all had personal bests, and we all wanted to do a bit better than before. We wanted to prove to ourselves that we could do well.

Did Satan want Jesus to prove Himself to everyone who might see Him throw Himself down from the pinnacle of the temple and not crash-land but be carried by angels? Whatever this "pinnacle" was, it was a height from which to fall would be disastrous. Does the temptation include a dependence on angels? Is it to *use* the angels for show?

What is a temptation?

To be tempted is to be *pressured* into doing something you otherwise might never do. It is to be *lured, enticed, seduced, tantalized*. To be tempted is to be *baited*, a fishing term. And that sort of bait is often a treat that disguises a hook—a sharp, barbed hook! John Bevere wrote a book entitled *The Bait of Satan*, where he speaks of how the devil uses little spats in churches that members are tempted to let become big issues to them and which can make the whole congregation become entirely ineffective. In fact, sometimes the Holy Spirit absents itself from such congregations. Sometimes the temptation comes in the form of something very attractive … at first. Sometimes it is the appeal of a certain sort of characteristic that draws people, as in "If I smoke, I will be cool," or "If I wear a low-cut blouse, I will be prettier."

Using the Angels

Have you ever been used by someone? You might have had a friend who mooched off you. You might have felt that you were being used by the girl you liked because she could "take advantage" of your kindness. You might be used by your company as just another cog in a big wheel. Your favor and friendship might just be someone's way of getting closer to the "boss" or to someone they liked better. Examples could go on forever. Whenever there is a quid pro quo, it can seem like you're being used.

Part of the devil's second temptation of Jesus in the wilderness is to use the angels. Would that be wrong? The angels *are* at Christ's command. But Satan wanted Jesus to use them in order to either prove Himself or to show off. The first temptation was for Jesus to feed Himself by turning a stone into bread. But Jesus proclaims that the human body does not live by bread alone (Matthew 4:4). The fact is that we are more than just bodies. We are souls. And our souls must be fed. Feeding the soul is just as important as feeding the body … though we are tempted to believe that we don't really need to feed the soul that much or that regularly. In each temptation, the devil is enticing Christ to use His power—for Himself, for show, and for wealth. If Jesus fed Himself, would it have been a sin? Or would it be a sin to transform the stone? A debate for another time, perhaps.

Note right now that *it is not a sin to be tempted*! Temptations only become sinful when you give in. To tempt another, though, *is* a sinful act. We cannot completely avoid temptation, but we can pray for God to lead us away from it and to be delivered from evil. Martin Luther once said that "You can't keep the birds from flying overhead, but you can keep them from building a nest in your hair!" Seems like a life-giving truth (LGT).

Temptations have always been around. It was even in the Garden of Eden (Genesis 3:6). Later, east of Eden, Cain was downcast because what he had given as an offering to God was not looked upon favorably. God told Cain, "Why are you angry? … If you do well, will you not be accepted? And if you do not do well, sin is lurking at the door; it's desire is for you, but you must master it" (Genesis4:6–7). "Sin is lurking at the door!" Like a predatory animal, the temptation to sin needs to be mastered. Peter said, "Discipline yourselves. Keep alert. Like a roaring lion your adversary (the word *Satan* means *adversary*) the devil prowls around, looking for someone to devour. Resist him, steadfast in your faith, for you know that your brothers and sisters in all the world are undergoing the same kinds of suffering" (1 Peter 5:8–9). Never think that you are completely alone in the ways you are being tempted. No one is immune. (LGT)

And in the Letter to the Hebrews, we are told, "We do not have a high priest who is unable to sympathize with our weaknesses, but we have one who in every respect has been tempted as we are, yet without sin ... Let us therefore approach the throne of grace with boldness, so that we may receive mercy and find grace to help in times of need" (Hebrews 4:15, 16). Jesus was tempted. But He did not sin. Jesus knows our every weakness because He experienced them Himself! Luther taught that there are three kinds of temptation: fleshly, worldly, and of the devil. And he said, "To be left alone ... then I am in that school, and I can learn what I am, how weak my faith is ..." But in 1540, he wrote, "In the worst temptations nothing can help us but faith that God's Son has put on flesh, is bone, sits at the right hand of the Father, and prays for us. There is no mightier comfort."

Being tempted humbles us. It can remind us of our desperate need for a savior. Peter spoke of the trials of temptation in his first letter, saying,

> Now for a little while you have had to suffer various trials, so that the genuineness of your faith – being more precious than gold, which though perishable, is tested by fire – may be found to result in praise and glory and honor when Jesus Christ is revealed. Although you have not seen him, you love him; and even though you do not see him now, you believe in him and rejoice with an indescribable and glorious joy, for you are receiving the outcome of your faith, the salvation of your souls (1 Peter 1:6–9).

Later, in that letter, Peter said, "Do not be surprised at the painful trial you are suffering as though something strange were happening to you. But rejoice that you participate in the sufferings of Christ, so that you may be overjoyed when his glory is revealed" (4:12–13).

Peter was focusing on the persecution of Christians. In the New International Version, "painful trials" is translated as a "fiery ordeal" (1 Peter 4:12 NIV). The trials, tests, and purpose of it all was to prove their faith. The first temptation in such circumstances comes through the instinct of self-preservation—to run, flee from the persecution rather than to stand firm in Christ. If you don't run, you would be tempted to deny your faith and save your skin. But … that would be to lose your soul! Either way, it is an exercise in escape. And escape is not what God always wants.

When we suffer, either physically or emotionally, we will want to escape. Often we are tempted to numb the pain or escape from it into some sort of false high. We don't want to feel the pain. We don't want to have to struggle. But to use drugs or alcohol or to pursue behaviors that give only temporary pleasure leaves an easy opening for the devil to really get her hooks in us. And nobody really wants that. Rick Warren, in *The Purpose-Driven Life*, said that "temptations begin by capturing your attention." But … when we pursue a behavior only because it feels good, we can get caught hook, line, and sinker by what is called the pleasure principle—"if it feels good, do it." But to do it without any regard to the consequences that may result is foolish. It is sin. (LGT)

If You Are the Son of God

The devil tempted Jesus by suggesting He was not what He knew He was, "If you are the Son of God …" The idea was that the devil wanted Jesus to question His very nature, His essence. He was hungry, famished, vulnerable, probably even physically weak. In His humanness, He was in agony. He needed food, but He had already resisted the devil's first temptation. He knew that no one lives by bread alone. Jesus knew the Word of God. This fed Him more than anything. It can feed us too.

But then the devil used Jesus's own method of self-defense against Him; she quoted scripture! The devil quoted two promises about divine protection: "He will command his angels concerning you," and "On their hands they will bear you up, so that you will not dash your foot against a stone." Both are from Psalm 91:11–12. Surely that got Jesus's attention. Scripture is often used to make a point and too often used to judge people. And though that is not always wrong, the Bible is not meant to be a weapon to assassinate someone's character. It should more often be a source of hope and encouragement. (LGT)

Here, it is used to tempt Jesus. I think the devil is tempting Jesus to use the divine power in His life to do something spectacular. Jesus wouldn't have needed to do this for Himself but in order to get recognition from His fans! Jesus has kept His messianic abilities virtually hidden until now. And then during His ministry, He would get little recognition from the religious leaders in Jerusalem. As much as we might like the sort of recognition that tempts us to do something amazing, we shouldn't be so ego-driven that we *need* to do such things. Doing something magical, like pretending to turn water into wine by using potassium permanganate, is cool, and the children can be impressed by you when you do it as an object lesson for a children's message, but do not suggest that you used some kind of divine power. That would be just plain wrong.

So … showing off, not wise, especially for Jesus. Being tempted to doubt Himself, not possible. Jesus resisted, and so can we.

Scriptures

To discover more about what the Bible says about being humble, here are some scripture passages that will help to inspire us:

2 Chronicles 7:16 – If my people who are called by my name humble themselves, pray, seek my face, and turn from their wicked ways, then I will hear from heaven, and will forgive their sin and heal their land.

Psalm 131:1–2 – O Lord, my heart is not lifted up, my eyes are not raised too high; I do not occupy myself with things too great and too marvelous for me. But I have calmed and quieted my soul, like a weaned child with its mother, my soul is like the weaned child.

Psalm 149:4 – For the Lord takes pleasure in his people; he adorns the humble with victory.

Proverbs 3:34 – Toward the scorners he is scornful, but to the humble he shows favor.

Proverbs 15:33 – The fear of the Lord is instruction in wisdom, and humility goes before honor.

Proverbs 16:18–19 – Pride goes before destruction, and a haughty spirit before a fall. It is better to be of a lowly spirit among the poor than to divide the spoil with the proud.

Micah 6:8 – Walk humbly with your God.

Zechariah 9:9 – Rejoice greatly, O daughter Zion! Shout aloud, O daughter Jerusalem! Lo, your king comes to you; triumphant and victorious is he, humble and riding on a donkey, on a colt, the foal of a donkey.

Matthew 5:3 – Blessed are the poor in spirit, for theirs is the kingdom of heaven.

Matthew 5:5 – Blessed are the meek, for they will inherit the earth.

Matthew 11:29 – Take my yoke upon you, and learn from me; for I am gentle and humble in heart, and you will find rest for your souls.

Matthew 18:4 – Whoever becomes humble like this child is the greatest in the kingdom of heaven.

Matthew 23:8–12 – All who exalt themselves will be humbled, and all who humble themselves will be exalted.

Romans 12:3 – For by the grace given to me I say to everyone among you not to think of yourselves more highly than you ought to think, but to think with sober judgment, each according to the measure of faith that God has assigned.

Romans 12:11 – Do not lag in zeal, be ardent in spirit, serve the Lord.

Ephesians 4:1–3 – I therefore, the prisoner in the Lord, beg you to lead a life worthy of the calling to which you have been called, with all humility and gentleness, with patience, bearing with one another in love, making every effort to maintain the unity of the Spirit in the bond of peace.

Philippians 2:3–4 – Do nothing from selfish ambition or conceit, but in humility regard others as better than yourselves.

James 4:10 – Humble yourselves before the Lord and he will exalt you.

1 Peter 3:8 – Finally, all of you, have unity of spirit, sympathy, love for one another, a tender heart, and a humble mind.

1 Peter 5:6–7 – Humble yourselves therefore under the mighty hand of God, so that he may exalt you in due time.

What to Do

- Prove your faith, not yourself. Christ is in you!
- Don't show off. Don't try to be something you're not.
- Be humble.
- Think of how you might be enticed by the desire for recognition.
- Think about the ways the devil gets your attention. What are the lures? How do you resist them?
- Build a wall of faith around yourself. Let scripture be your stronghold.
- Admit your weaknesses to yourself. Build your strength at those points. Resistance training!
- Don't question your faith. Trust it.
- Realize that it is not a sin to be tempted. The sin is giving in.
- Don't just try to escape. Fight. Resist!
- Think: What encourages you when you feel tested? Go there often.
- Don't give up.

A Prayer

Almighty God, make me meek enough to be humble and wise enough to serve Your kingdom. Let the power of Your Spirit in me give me grace to defend myself from the lures of the devil, and by Word of truth, guard my heart and mind in faith. This I ask in Jesus's name. Amen.

A Poem

Is There a Way

Is there a way that I can prove
My love for you is still sincere?
Then let me simply try to move
Closer to you now and here.
Let me tell you I am yours,
And let me gaze into your eyes
And say how you have opened doors
In my heart when it starts to rise
With wings your beauty can inspire
And how my soul begins to soar
And how you set my mind on fire
And how I wish time could be more …
But you are gone. You can't come back.
Your tender touch is what I lack.

CHAPTER FOUR

———◇◆◇———

DON'T TEMPT
GOD

Jesus said to him,
"Again it is written,
'Do not put the Lord your God to the test.'"
—MATTHEW 4:7

There are many ways temptation gets to us. When we begin to take things for granted, we can easily be tempted to neglect their relevance in our lives. It happens in relationships, it happens in social circumstances, it happens at church, and it happens with respect to the law. People fall into complacency or indifference or immorality. One excuse we're often tempted to use in our defense is "I'm only human!" or "I couldn't help myself!" Excuuuuse me! When we become believers, we put off our old self, which is, in fact, only human, and we clothe ourselves with Christ! He becomes our source of power. His will is working in our lives. We can resist!

In 1 Corinthians 10:12–13, Paul wrote, "If you think you are standing, watch out that you do not fall. No temptation has overtaken you that is not common to everyone. God is faithful, and he will not let you be tested beyond your strength, but with the temptation he will provide the way out so that you may be able to endure it." God will provide a way. His way is in His Word. That's what Jesus used again to resist the devil.

Confidence in the Word is a great enabler. If Jesus was tempted to feel humble, He was already there: "The Son of Man came not to be served, but to serve …" (Mark 10:45a). "I am gentle and humble in heart …" (Matthew 11:29) If He was tempted to use the angels, well, He already knew His purpose was to give Himself, He would "give his life a ransom for many" (Mark 10:45b). And certainly, it would just be absurd for Him to show off by doing something so spectacular as to seem to fly.

His resistance for this second temptation in the wilderness was, in my mind, instant and stern: "Again it is written, 'Do not put the Lord your God to the test'" (Matthew 4:7). He's saying to the devil, "You can't tempt me!" He's saying, "Don't even try it."

James teaches us well concerning temptation. He says, "My brothers and sisters, whenever you face various trials of any kind, consider it nothing but joy, because you know that the testing of your faith produces endurance; and let endurance have its full effect, so that you may be mature and complete, lacking nothing. If any of you is lacking wisdom, ask God, who gives to all generously and ungrudgingly, and it will be given you" (James 1:2–3). (LGT)

As far as Jesus is concerned, He knew this. He was already complete, He was wise. This effort in temptation had become a teaching experience for the devil. The devil was being schooled.

"Blessed is anyone who endures temptation. Such a one has stood the test and will receive the crown of life that the Lord has promised to those who love him. No one, when tempted, should say, 'I am being tempted by God'; for God tempts no one. But one is tempted by one's own desire, being lured and enticed by it; then, when that desire has conceived, it gives birth to sin, and that sin, when it is fully grown, gives birth to death" (James 1:12–15).

Obviously, there is a difference between being tempted to sin and being tested by God to discover His strength in our lives. The Israelites were "tested" in the wilderness after the Exodus. They were not ready to enter the promised land. It would take forty years of "testing." They needed to learn to trust God and God's provision, as in water from the rock and manna for food. If Jesus is being "tested" by the devil, He is passing easily. That's why there can be joy because we too can pass the devil's tests. And we too will receive a crown of life. Jesus already had His.

"Submit yourselves therefore to God. Resist the devil and he will flee from you. Draw near to God, and he will draw near to you. Cleanse your hands, you sinners, and purify your hearts, you double-minded. Lament and mourn and weep. Let your laughter be turned into mourning and your joy into dejection. Humble yourselves before the Lord, and he will exalt you" (James 4:7–10). Big life-giving truth there!

James is telling us to take our temptations seriously, to realize our need for God. Resistance comes by the Word, and the Word comes by grace. God cannot be tempted by evil. One of the greatest temptations we face as humans is to call evil good, to say it's okay to sin a little bit. To think this way is to tempt God because God is good all the time. And God does not abide any evil.

I like the idea that when we resist the devil, he flees from us. Before the strength of faith, the devil is weak. The devil doesn't just give up, he flees! He has to escape. We need to see the reality of sin through this lens. We need to build the strength of faith in our lives. We are weaker without the Word of scripture. We need to learn it. We need to share it, study it, and know it well. (LGT)

How do we do that? Read the Bible. Read it with friends. Hear it in worship. Every sermon should be based on scripture. Not every sermon will be expositional, teaching a passage word for word, but every sermon you hear should bring a deeper understanding of what the Bible says. To neglect to worship is one of the temptations everyone faces. We take the need to worship for granted. It becomes too routine for us, or we become complacent. Sometimes we think we know enough. We tend to water down the sincerity we started with by feeling overconfident or proud. We can become arrogant. That's why we need endurance. We need to be steadfast!

I have known many who felt that after experiencing saving

grace and the conviction of faith, that was all they needed. Some continued to worship because they felt obligated, and because they did so, they experienced many more moments of awakening and resolve. They grew, and they were inspired. But sadly, too many drift away from worship. It's as if they felt as though they had graduated from church, that they didn't need it anymore. They had been justified; they had their ticket to heaven. But ... there is such a thing as sanctifying grace, the working of God in our lives that makes us holy, that helps us grow, that inspires us to carry on in faith, that even makes us want to serve somehow. It gives us a witness that others may learn from.

Sometimes it is a negative experience of some kind that sets us adrift. Either something turned them off, let them down, or made them feel bad, sad, or depressed. I didn't want to worship for a while after my first girlfriend broke up with me. We always sat together at church. It didn't last long because of my resolve to worship. I still loved God and wanted more from Jesus. It was more important to me to be faithful than to look like I had a girlfriend. But it sure felt good to have a girlfriend. Was that a temptation?

When we learn that "the testing of your faith produces endurance," we are able to discern the source of our endurance. I mentioned "resistance training." Weightlifters don't start out with the heaviest weights there are. They exercise with smaller weights, adding more weight when their muscles have grown. Resistance training involves straining the muscles. That tears them down a bit, but with a little rest, the muscles rebuild themselves, and they are stronger. The weightlifter's muscles become resistant to the strain, and when they add some weight, even if it's just two more pounds, they can do it. Soon enough, they've gone from 100 pounds to 120. And they are stronger. Likewise, runners don't start out running 10 miles, they add more distance after several days. Training. Building up. Resistance. Faith can be like that. We may not feel the progress as we aim at heavier weights or greater distances, but in time, we will realize that we have gained "endurance."

We may not conquer all our temptations right away, but we can defeat them one by one, bit by bit, until we are able to "let endurance have its full effect so that you may be mature and complete, lacking nothing." We're not building muscle, but we're becoming more mature.

Sadly, the devil often returns with a new temptation, and we need to do some more enduring.

Scripture

Because confidence comes from encouragement, here are some scripture passages on encouragement that will help to inspire us:

Psalm 25:8–9 – Good and upright is the Lord; therefore he instructs sinners in the way. He leads the humble in what is right, and teaches the humble his way.

Psalm 32:1 – Happy are those whose transgression is forgiven, whose sin is covered.

Psalm 86:15 – But you, O Lord, are a God merciful and gracious, slow to anger and abounding in steadfast love and faithfulness.

Psalm 103:2–5 – Bless the Lord, O my soul, and do not forget his benefits – who forgives iniquity, who heals our diseases, who redeems your life from the Pit, who crowns you with steadfast love and mercy, who satisfies you with good as long as you live so that your youth is renewed like the eagle's.

Psalm 103:12–13 – As far as the east is from the west, so far he removes our transgression from us. As a father has compassion for his children, so the Lord has compassion for those who fear him.

Matthew 6:14 – For if you forgive others their trespasses, your heavenly Father will also forgive you.

Matthew 6:15 – But if you do not forgive others, neither will your Father forgive your trespasses.

TOM KINGERY

Matthew 9:13 – Go and learn what this means, "I desire mercy, not sacrifice." For I have come to call not the righteous but sinners.

Luke 5:32 – I have come to call not the righteous but sinners to repentance.

Luke 6:37 – Do not judge, and you will not be judged; do not condemn, and you will not be condemned. Forgive, and you will be forgiven.

Romans 5:8 – God proves his love for us in that while we were sinners Christ died for us.

Ephesians 4:32 – Be kind to one another, tenderhearted, forgiving one another, as God in Christ has forgiven you.

Colossians 1:13–14 – He has rescued us from the power of darkness and transferred us into the kingdom of his beloved Son, in whom we have redemption, the forgiveness of sins.

Colossians 3:13 – Bear with one another and, if anyone has a complaint against another, forgive each other; just as the Lord has forgiven you, so you also must forgive.

Hebrews 8:12 – "For I will be merciful toward their iniquities, and I will remember their sins no more."

1 John 1:9 – If we confess our sins, he who is faithful will forgive us our sins and cleanse us from all unrighteousness.

What to Do

> Don't take your faith nor worship for granted.
> Let yourself be clothed with Christ. What does that mean to you? Have you put off your "old self"?
> Humble yourself.
> Be confident in your faith and in the Word.
> Build up your endurance.

- Be wise. On a scale of 1–10, 10 being very wise and 1 being unwise, how would you rank yourself?
- Consider the desires that lure you into temptation. What are they?
- Draw near to God.
- Read the Bible. Know the Word.
- Consider the ways and reasons people drift away from regular worship.
- Try to defeat your temptations one at a time.

A Prayer

Almighty God, Your word is encouragement and strength; the more I know it, the greater my strength will be. Give me grace for my journey. Help me to remember that You are with me always. And let my confidence in Your way rub off on others so that they may find encouragement as well. This I pray in Jesus's name. Amen.

A Song

We Will All Dream Together
Tune: "Wild Mountain Thyme"

O the time is surely coming
When the storm will prove the heart
And the sky will be the limit
When the clouds begin to part
Will you stay with me there

Refrain:
And we'll all dream together
Of a perfect rising sun
When the morning lasts forever
And the day is never done
Will you stay with me there

Will we build a love unfailing
Will we build a memory
Will it send our ships a-sailing
Will we build a soul that's free
Will you stay with me there

Refrain …
If I find your name engraved in stone
Well, it doesn't mean a thing
I'll just wander to the hills alone
Drink cool water from the spring
And you'll be with me there

Refrain …
We took Jesus as our Savior
A long, long time away
So I'll see you in the sunrise
Of every single day
You are always with me there

Refrain …
O the time is surely coming
When the storm will prove the heart
And the sky will be the limit
When the clouds begin to part
Will you be with me there

Refrain …

CHAPTER FIVE

WORSHIP ME

Again the devil took him to a very high mountain
and showed him all the kingdoms of the world and their splendor;
and he said to him,
"All these I will give you,
if you will fall down and worship me."
—MATTHEW 4:8–9

Another "If …"

There is a sort of temptation that often comes before us that actually looks good … at first. It's the temptation to take a shortcut. Kids want to take the shortcut through a neighbor's yard. Youth want to take the shortcut to adulthood and adult behavior. We all want shortcuts to love, to wealth, to status, and to heaven. But … "the gate is wide and the way is easy that leads to destruction, and many enter through it. But the gate is narrow and the way is hard that leads to life, and only a few find it!" (Matthew 7:13–14; LGT)

We are often tempted to take the easier way. And often it has to do with cheating or sidestepping the rules. Few people actually like doing everything the hard way, but that's the only real way. Jesus was tempted by the devil to worship him. To paraphrase what the devil said, "All you have to do is worship me, and you will have it all!" First of all, "all the kingdoms of the world and their splendor" were not the devil's to give. So the devil is lying, trying to trick Jesus. All the splendor of all the kingdoms belong to the people of those kingdoms. "If …"

Second, the temptation is not really about worldly wealth or status, though these things are often the desires that lure us into sin. It's about worship. Take away the enticements and all the devil is saying is "Worship me." The question becomes more poignant when you are a believer and a part of a community of faith, and the opportunity to worship presents itself, but you choose to do something else. Before whom or what have you bowed down? Idolatry is the most common sin of all because anything that takes God's place in our lives becomes our god.

Teilhard de Chardin, a theologian of the twentieth century, has said that whatever your *ultimate concern* is that becomes your god! For many people, Sunday morning is a time for comfort and ease (rest). So going to worship seems optional. But the fourth commandment is to "Remember the Sabbath (as a day of rest) to *keep it holy!*" The purpose of Sabbath Day is worship. Yes, we rest from our labors … in order to rest in God's presence. We are to focus on faith. "If …" (LGT)

We are tempted to think we've gotten our ticket, we've experienced saving grace, we're okay. We want the shortcut version of faith, what Dietrich Bonhoeffer called *cheap grace*. Well, now realize that God isn't finished with you yet. You're coming to worship is not only for your own good, but that someone else might also be blessed by your presence when the opportunity for worship arises in your community of faith.

For some, Sunday morning, or whenever your community of faith worships, might actually be a time to work. Their place of employment calls on them to work when they should be worshiping. Well, you can't serve both God and money! (Matthew 6:24) This needs to be qualified, however. We desperately need health-care workers to be able to work even on Sundays. When the opportunity to worship arises, they need to work. But … no one is absolutely required to work every single Sunday, so when they are free to come to worship, what should

God expect? What should the church, the worshipping community, expect? The same goes for police, farmers, soldiers, and government workers. What does God want? What lures you away from worship … every Sunday?

For some, their absence from worship might have something to do with sporting events! They might be participants on the team, or they might be spectators. This is shameful in so many ways because the coordinators of such events use the excuse that "It's the only time we could schedule the games!" False! Priorities are being confused in such circumstances. And Jesus said, "Seek first (as in priority) God's kingdom and God's righteousness, and all else will be yours as well" (Matthew 6:33). (LGT)

Jesus was speaking about the things that cause us to worry anxiously when He says this. And one of the ways the devil often works is to distract us with things that are less important, making us unfocused and unfruitful. Sometimes to worry is to be tempted to focus on things in counterproductive ways. It is not a sin to make plans. But when you've got plans, and you fret anxiously about carrying out the details before they can even begin to fall into place, we are leaning in the direction of sin. And when we worry about health or wealth or relationships, when otherwise we could pray and place these things in God's hands, again, we are leaning toward sin. It is sin because we are not trusting God … when we should. "If …"

For most human beings, the devil comes along and whispers little suggestions, and you're lured away. "We are tempted by our own desire, being lured and enticed by it" (James 1:14). With humor, people often say, "The devil made me do it." But no one can make you do anything you don't want to do. Use a little self-control! It's a fruit of the Spirit! If we don't blame the devil for our sin, we might use the excuse for giving in by admitting, "I'm weak," or "I was weak, I couldn't refuse." There's another lie we tell ourselves because Paul was told that "God's power is made perfect in weakness" (2 Corinthians 12:9b). God told him, "My grace is sufficient for you" (2 Corinthians 12:9a). (Big LGT)

Remember, "God is faithful, and He will not let you be tempted beyond your strength, but with the testing He will provide the way out so that you may be able to endure it" (1 Corinthians 10:12–13). God is on our side. God is our strength. God will provide a way. Not a shortcut! God provides a way, and Jesus Christ is the Way! (John 14:6)

Our focus, our purpose, our primary thought, our priority should be Deuteronomy 6:13: "Worship the Lord your God, and serve only him!" Jesus repeated it to the devil! We believe it! That settles it! "Seek first God's kingdom and God's righteousness!"

Scriptures

To discover more about what the Bible says about idolatry, here are some scripture passages that will help us to understand:

Exodus 20:3–6 – You shall have no other gods before me. You shall not make for yourself an idol, whether in the form of anything that is in heaven above, or that is on the earth beneath, or that is in the water under the earth. You shall not bow down to them or worship them; for I the Lord your God am a jealous God, punishing children for the iniquity of parents, to the third and the fourth generation of those who reject me, but showing steadfast love to the thousandth generation of those who love me and keep my commandments.

Exodus 23:13 – Do not invoke the names of other gods; do not let them be heard on your lips.

Leviticus 19:4 – Do not turn to idols or make cast images for yourselves: I am the Lord your God.

Deuteronomy 13:3 – You must not heed the words of those prophets or those who divine dreams; for the Lord your God is testing you, to know whether you will indeed love the Lord your God with all your heart and soul.

1 Samuel 15:23 – For rebellion is no less a sin than divination, and stubbornness is like iniquity and idolatry. Because you have rejected the word of the Lord, he has rejected you from being king.

1 Kings 18:26 – (The story of the contest between Elijah and the prophets of Baal on Mount Carmel) So they took the bull that was given them, prepared it, and called on the name of Baal from morning until noon, crying, "O Baal, answer us!" But there was no voice, and no answer. They limped about the altar that they made.

Psalm 96:5 – For all the gods of the people are idols, but the Lord made the heavens.

Psalm 135:15–18 – The idols of the nations are silver and gold, the work of human hands. They have mouths, but they do not speak; they have eyes, but they do not see; they have ears, but they do not hear, and there is no breath in their mouths. Those who make them and all who trust them shall become like them.

Isaiah 46:7 – They lift it to their shoulders, they carry it, they set it in its place, and it stands there; it cannot move from its place. If one cries out to it, it does not answer or save anyone from trouble.

Micah 5:13 – And I will cut off your images and your pillars from among you, and you shall bow down no more to the work of your hands …

Jonah 2:8 – Those who worship vain idols forsake their true loyalty.

Habakkuk 2:18 – What is an idol once its maker has shaped it—a cast image, a teacher of lies? For its maker trusts in what has been made, though the product is only an idol that cannot speak.

Acts 17:16 – While Paul was waiting for them in Athens, he was deeply distressed to see that the city was full of idols.

Acts 17:29 – Since we are God's offspring, we ought not to think that the deity is like gold, or silver, or stone, an image formed by the art and imagination of mortals.

Galatians 4:8 – Formerly, when you did not know God, you were enslaved to beings that by nature are not gods.

Colossians 3:5 – Put to death, therefore, whatever in you is earthly: fornication, impurity, passion, evil desire, and greed (which is idolatry).

What to Do

- Substitute nothing for worship nor for God.
- Beware of idols!
- Think of the shortcuts you've been tempted to take.
- Think about the idea of the sabbath. Is it only a day of rest, or is it a day for worship?
- Consider: When might it be justifiable to miss worship? What if you're sick?
- Consider the things that make you anxious, that make you worry. How does temptation come at such times?
- Consider statues or sculptures. What is it about them that makes what they represent seem real?
- Practice self-control.

A Prayer

Almighty God, May my worship bring You honor. May my love for Your Son give me strength. And may my steadfast hope in Your Word stir my mind and heart to live and work for Your purposes. Always. I ask this prayer in Jesus's name. Amen.

A Poem

Be My First Thought

Be my first thought, O God, when I rise.
You are the sunlight that opens my eyes.
You are the air in each breath that I take.
And You are a part of the plans that I make.

May all that I am and all that I do
Be done for Your Kingdom, O Lord, and for You.
I give You myself and my soul and my heart;
And my mind, it is Yours, every thought every part.

And though I am far from what I should be
Let me press on 'til You're finished with me.
You've brought me this far and it's not over yet.
Defeat every hindrance. Conquer each threat
And pour out Your Spirit, Your love, and Your grace
And give me Your peace 'til I finish my race.

CHAPTER SIX

WORSHIP GOD

Jesus said to him,
"Away with you, Satan!
For it is written,
'worship the Lord your God, and serve only him.'"
—MATTHEW 4:10

True worship honors God. It glorifies God.

When we want to honor someone for some accomplishment or act of bravery, we want to do something that is special. There are medals and awards, there are symbols we use to express appreciation and exceptional gratitude. Meanwhile, all God wants is our presence. To worship is to present ourselves before the presence of God. But when we present ourselves to God, God will often accept us, take us, and use us. God is honored when we come to Him. And God is glorified when we praise Him, serve Him, and love Him. (LGTs)

Our worship inspires our ministry and mission. I have said that ministry is what we do in and for the church, while mission reaches beyond the church where we are needed and where Christ would have us go. Being immersed in mission and ministry helps us resist temptation. Being involved is not a distraction, necessarily, from the wrong activities we might be tempted to gravitate toward; but a plan, a focus, a purpose in the right direction. I like what C. S. Lewis said, "Aim at heaven and you get earth thrown in. Aim at earth and you get neither." When we have positive purposes in our lives, we will have a lot less time for the negative possibilities. It's about doing the right thing. James has said that "whoever knows the right thing to do and fails to do it, is guilty of sin" (James 4:17). (LGT) There is always the temptation in life to be negligent. Opportunities to serve can easily be missed when we are distracted by the temptation to do something else. Part of what we need is a community that nurtures our involvement. That's why the church can be helpful when we need to resist temptations. We have helpers, and we can be helpers.

Jesus was alone in the wilderness though. No one could help Him. Well, maybe He wasn't alone. We need to remember that both God and the Holy Spirit were with Him, part of Him. Jesus is God in three persons, the blessed Trinity! But Jesus was also so immersed in the Word that He defied the devil: "Away with you, Satan! For it is written, 'Worship the Lord your God, and serve only him'" (Matthew 4:10). (LGT) We, who believe, also have the Holy Spirit. Sadly, though, we are not always *in* the Spirit when we need to be.

The *adversary*! I have said that the name *Satan* literally means *adversary*. Jesus calls the devil Satan. An adversary is often anyone who is against us. Certainly, Satan was against Jesus. But Satan is so against Jesus that he also goes after His followers.

When we are tempted, we need to let the Spirit of Christ move in us in order to resist the devil. We need to let the Word of truth manifest itself in our hearts and minds. And we can have a posture of resistance. Long, long ago, I dated a girl only one time, who kept on trying to get me do something more intimate than I was willing to do. I simply told her, "I'm not like that." I knew enough about myself, my moral values and standards, that I wasn't about to behave affectionately before it was right. I was probably more proud of myself than I should have been because I said no. But I did resist. And it wasn't entirely easy. It was at a time when I was fairly newly convicted to want to go into the ministry. I confess that I did imagine a few times what would have happened if I had taken advantage of her advances. Sorry to say. Resist!

We need a similar posture about worship. We don't want to miss it because we're "not like that!" We *want* to honor God. We want to be so involved that nothing can change our plans when the time for worship comes, except on rare occasions. And when we are so immersed, we will love righteousness too much to let unrighteous activity have a chance to lure us away. (LGT) Resist by what you insist in doing. Resist and insist.

The devil will promise us anything and everything. Tempters offer us more than they're really willing to give just to get us to do what they want us to do. We want to fit in, but if we don't want to go along with the crowd that promises welcome, we'll often be rejected. In my teen years, I liked playing my guitar with others. I was hungry to learn riffs and chord progressions. Several of us would gather at one guy's house and teach one another what we knew. It was fun. But it often spiraled down into immoral conversations and drug use. That was when I knew it was time for me to exit. They welcomed me at first. They knew I wanted to become a minister one day, but my moral standards again couldn't let me go where they wanted to go.

Moral maturity was hard to come by among many of my friends. Maybe I was ahead of my age in that regard. But God had gotten ahold of me. Maybe I became a little condescending when I refused to go along. I was accused of being jealous because I was the least musical among them, so they had an excuse to exclude me. But I did learn a lot from those guys, and for that, I was grateful. The promise of stardom in the world of rock music wasn't that realistic anyway. That wasn't the real appeal anyway; it was, for me, a vehicle for my poetry and lyrics. As it turned out, the only lyrics I ever created the music for was the song that was sung at our wedding. And everybody there liked it. It was only played once, and it wasn't recorded. Still, though, it often plays in my head.

Big visions, like the splendor of all the kingdoms of the world, can entice us. But we need to be rational. We need to know what is realistic. None of my friends became rock stars, and I wonder what happened to many of those players of my young adulthood. But I don't feel like I missed anything. I had found the greatest treasure of all: faith.

Being a Christian is the best prevention against behavior that is contrary to the kingdom of God. (LGT) It doesn't remove temptation completely, but it gives us a posture of strength and righteousness.

Lot lived in Sodom. The people were wicked, and Lot found it hard to connect. Some of the men came to gang up on the angelic visitors that came into his home. Lot went out to talk them out of such wicked behavior. And when the Sodomites were about to have their way with Lot, the angels pulled him back inside and blinded the evil Sodomites (Genesis 19:1–11). Later, when these angels told Lot to gather his family and flee from Sodom because they were going to destroy the city, they told them to go and not look back. When God rained sulfur and fire on both Sodom and Gomorrah, Lot's wife looked back. Doing so turned her into a pillar of salt (Genesis 19:12–26).

Looking back can be a tempting thing. I think we all like to play the game of "What if?" What if I wasn't so sensitive about the moral disrespect of my friends? What if I had joined in their drug use? What if? Well, I don't care and never really did. I made my choices, and I'm so glad I did. Eventually, I was happy in my ministry in the United Methodist Church. I was very happy to have met Carol when I did. I am glad we married, and I am proud of my children and all they are accomplishing. There may be some things I would change, if I could go back, but what has happened has still brought blessings. I would change Carol's illness in an instant. I would love for her to still be alive today. But I should never want to take her triumph away. She is in eternity now, and I will see her again someday. I do look back to remember the blessings I have known. But I'm smart enough to know that I can't change anything. I am not really tempted to change anything. And I don't like to think of the foolish things I've done. But memories can make us happy. They can make us strong. They can remind us of all the ways God *has* been with us.

Could part of this third temptation in the wilderness be the temptation to have power? I think so. What if … Jesus had accepted the power the devil tried to offer? People seem to enjoy being the boss. Business and politics open the door to power. Being able to rule over others has an appeal. If you have power, you can make people do almost anything you want. Blackmailing someone or ransoming hostages seems like wielding a sort of power. It is oppressive, though, so it is obviously sinful, and we should never go there. The positive side of authoritative power is being responsible. Jesus was responsible with His power.

He told a parable about power and responsibility. It's called "The Parable of the Talents," and it's in the Gospel of Matthew 25:14–30. Three different servants were each given the financial resources to accomplish something while the master was absent. Two did right by the master, one did nothing. The master responds to the good work of the two by telling them, "Well done, good and trustworthy slave; you have been trustworthy in a few things, I will put you in charge of many things; enter into the joy of your master" (Matthew 25:21, 23). And in the conclusion of the parable, Jesus tells the moral of the story: "To all those who have, will more be given, and they will have an abundance" (Matthew 25:29a).

To those who have ... What? Wisdom, wealth, understanding? Perhaps, but my answer is responsibility. To those who have the character trait of responsibility, more responsibility will be given! The goal is not just to be rich, but to honor the master. The purpose is not to control others. Wanting to have "power" over others is a temptation we need to resist. We resist it with love; love others as we'd want to be loved. Don't use people!

Jesus must have told His disciples about His temptations in the wilderness since they have become part of the Gospel stories written by Matthew, Mark, and Luke. But we can learn from what He endured.

Scriptures

To discover more about what the Bible says about worship, here are some scripture passages on that will help us to understand:

Exodus 23:25 – You shall worship the Lord your God, and he will bless your bread and water; and will take sickness away from you.

1 Chronicles 16:23–31 – Sing to the Lord, all the earth. Tell of his salvation from day to day. Declare his glory among the nations, his marvelous works among all the peoples. For great is the Lord, and greatly to

be praised; he is to be revered above all gods. For all the gods of the peoples are idols, but the Lord made the heavens. Honor and majesty are before him; strength and joy are in his place. Ascribe to the Lord, O families of the peoples, ascribe to the Lord glory and strength. Ascribe to the Lord the glory due his name, bring an offering, and come before him. Worship the Lord in holy splendor; tremble before him, all the earth. The world is firmly established; it shall never be moved. Let the heavens be glad, and let the earth rejoice, and let them say among the nations, "The Lord is king!"

1 Chronicles 16:34 – O give thanks to the Lord, for he is good; for his steadfast love endures forever.

Psalm 100:1–5 – Make a joyful noise to the Lord, all the earth. Worship the Lord with gladness; come into his presence with singing. Know that the Lord is God. It is he that made us, and we are his; we are his people, and the sheep of his pasture. Enter his gates with thanksgiving, and his courts with praise. Give thanks to him, bless his name. For the Lord is good, his steadfast love endures forever, and his faithfulness to all generations.

Psalm 150:6 – Let everything that has breath praise the Lord!

Isaiah 25:1 – O Lord, you are my God; I will exalt you, I will praise your name; for you have done wonderful things, plans formed of old, faithful and sure.

Isaiah 29:13–14a – The Lord said, "Because this people draw near with their mouths and honor me with their lips, while their hearts are far from me, and their worship of me is a human commandment learned by rote; so I will again do amazing things with this people, shocking and amazing ..."

Habakkuk 3:17–18 – Though the fig tree does not blossom, and no fruit is found on the vines; though the produce of the olive fails, and the fields yield no food; though the flock is cut off from the fold, and there is no herd in the stalls, yet I will rejoice in the Lord; I will exult in the God of my salvation.

Romans 11:36 – For from him and through him and to him are all things. To him be the glory forever. Amen.

Romans 12:1 – I appeal to you therefore, brothers and sisters, by the mercies of God, to present your bodies as a living sacrifice, holy and acceptable to the Lord, which is your spiritual worship.

Romans 14:11 – For it is written, "As I live, says the Lord, every knee shall bow before me, and every tongue shall give praise to God."

Hebrews 12:28–29 – Therefore, since we are receiving a kingdom that cannot be shaken, let us give thanks, by which we offer to God an acceptable worship with reverence and awe; for indeed our God is a consuming fire.

Revelation 4:9–11 – And whenever the living creatures give glory and honor and thanks to the one who is seated on the throne, who lives forever and ever, the twenty-four elders fall before the one who is seated on the throne and worship the one who lives forever and ever; they cast their crowns before the throne, singing, "You are worthy, our Lord and God, to receive glory and honor and power, for you created all things, and by your will they existed and were created."

What to Do

> Be a worshiper. Decide now what you will do when your community gathers for worship. Be there.
> Glorify God. Honor Christ. Celebrate faith. Give thanks. Be amazed.
> Find some way to serve God, whether it is through a committee at your church or a mission that is either local or far away. Be involved in what God is doing or wants to do. Consider the six possibilities in "The Parable of the Great Judgment" in Matthew 25.
> Know your purpose under God.

- Walk *in* the Spirit.
- Have a posture of resistance. In what circumstances might you be able to say, "I'm not like that"?
- Love righteousness too much to allow unrighteous ideas to be a lure.
- Don't look back. And don't play the game of "What if …?"
- Don't imagine that you can change the past. We can, however, change the ways we look at and interpret the past.
- Let your memories make you strong.
- Be responsible with what you have been given.

A Prayer

Almighty God, You invite us to enter Your throne room of grace, where we can ask and seek for Your will to be done. Please give us a posture of reverence and humility, for we know we're not truly worthy of You. But help us to present ourselves before You as Your subjects while Your reign over us is the power in our lives. We present our requests in our brokenness and need, and You listen to us in spite of ourselves. We thank You for this wonderful blessing, and we ask You to help us, always. This we ask in Jesus's name. Amen.

A Poem

Come, Let Us Share

Come, let us share all the treasure we've found.
Let us celebrate joyfully, cheerfully, glad
For the wonderful gifts we possess that abound
In the midst of the beautiful blessings we've had.

Let us give thanks and let us rejoice,
And let us remember the meaning it brings.
Let us bask in this pleasure. Let us lift up our voice,
Let our hearts overflow like a thousand fresh springs.

Come, let us share this great fire that burns
Where everyone offers some intangible fuel
By which others see and where everyone turns
And discovers the light and the passions that rule

Let us honor the goodness we feel with our friends.
And let us all echo our knowledge and grace
And let's call it a haven where bliss never ends
And where worship is true and where peace has a place

Let it seem as if time was just standing still
And all that we hope for God would fulfill

CONCLUSION

Submit yourselves therefore to God.
Resist the devil and he will from you.
—JAMES 4:7

Resisting the devil without having first submitted ourselves to God doesn't work that well. It's like running away from danger without having anything to run toward. You might just happen to run into another danger, maybe something worse. We need to know where to run. Run to Christ!

Jesus teaches submission by His example in the Garden of Gethsemane. In the Gospel of Luke, as Jesus prayed, He said, "Father, if you are willing, remove this cup from me; yet not my will but yours be done" (Luke 22:42). Paul teaches submission by what he says in Galatians 2:20: "It is no longer I who live, but Christ who lives in me." We relinquish ourselves and let Christ become alive in us. We remove ourselves and "put on the Lord Jesus Christ" (Romans 13:14). I think Joseph was surrendered when he found himself in Egypt as the slave of Potiphar. He bloomed where he was planted. The story is in Genesis 38. "The Lord was with Joseph, and he became a successful man" (v. 2). Long story short, Joseph was good at what he did and even became the second to the pharaoh (Genesis 41:40). Joseph surrendered himself to God, and God was able to work through him. (LGT)

We are to "submit ourselves to God" (James 4:7a). If it was dancing, God would lead. We would move where He wants us to go, and it would look right, feel right. When we give ourselves to God, God will do something with us. We can still be very purposeful, but it is within God's plans. We don't really lie down, we *stand* on His promises. God is our King, and we are His subjects. We are to humble ourselves and exalt God. (LGT)

In my career as a pastor in the United Methodist Church, I was appointed to serve several very different churches. When I had to move, I might have been in the middle of great programs and would have to leave them behind. It wasn't always easy, but I needed to be subject to the bishop and the cabinet and go where they thought I should go. And even then, in my new appointment, it was not *my* agenda that I served, but the agenda the new congregation called on me to attend to. I was subject to an appointment system. I had to be surrendered. So I understand what James is saying when he calls us to submit to God.

Submission is putting ourselves in God's hands. In God's hands, the grace to resist the devil is with us, in us. We are enabled because God cares about us. God wants us to be righteous, not sinful. God wants us to know *His* blessings, not the world's temptations. The more we submit to God, the more grace abounds in our lives. (LGTs)

Don't fear the devil. Love the Son. (LGTs) "Love conquers fear" (1 John 4:18). (LGT) We need to be so immersed in God's love that the devil just can't get to us. And should she try, we'll have the resources God gives us. We'll be able to call to mind the way we live by "every word that comes from the mouth of God" (Deuteronomy 8:3; Matthew 4:4).

Have confidence in Christ. His Spirit is in you because you believe. Let His Spirit reign in your heart and in your mind. Trust it. Be relinquished to the Holy Spirit. Submit, surrender, humble yourselves before Christ. Resistance is not automatic. It takes resolve to stand firm on the solid ground of faith. There will always be something that tries to send us off balance, but because of faith, with grace, we can correct ourselves. I like the idea of justifying the words in a paragraph, getting the margins straight. Typesetters, in the past, would set letters and words together to form paragraphs. If the typeset was "pied" (fallen, crooked, or disarrayed), putting it all back together was called justifying it. The confidence we have comes from the justifying work of Christ in our lives.

I think Isaac was surrendered when Abraham laid him on an altar to sacrifice him. Imagine the look in Isaac's eyes when he said, "Father ... the fire and the wood are here, but where is the lamb for a burnt offering?" (Genesis 22:7) He watched his father build an altar, set the wood in place, and then he let Abraham bind him and place him on the wood. Abraham raised his knife, but God stopped him from sacrificing his son. That was when Abraham discovered a ram caught in a thicket by its horns (Genesis 22:9–13). I want to believe Isaac had learned such trust, not only in Abraham, but in God as well, that God would provide. Why God would want to test Abraham in such a way has been debated by many scholars. I prefer the notion that Abraham needed to learn to trust in God for his future, rather than in Isaac.

God tests us sometimes. Not every test is a temptation. Sometimes they are just tests. "But with the testing he will also provide the way out so that you may be able to endure it" (1 Corinthians 10:13). That's how we can know it's a test from God. God also helps us in our temptations. And we know temptations to sin are often wrapped up in our own desires (James 1:14).

So ... James tells us, "Count it all joy ..." (James 1:2 NKJV) "My brothers and sisters, whenever you face trials of any kind, consider it nothing but joy, because you know that the testing of your faith produces endurance; and let endurance have its full effect, so that you may be mature and complete, lacking in nothing" (James 1:2–4). (LGT)

There's the reason for confidence. Resist the devil!

Scriptures

To discover more about what the Bible says about being submitted, here are some scripture passages that will help us to understand:

Job 22:21 NIV – "Submit to God and be at peace with him; in this way prosperity will come to you."

Psalm 95:6 – O come, let us worship and bow down, let us kneel before the Lord, our Maker.

Proverbs 3:5–7 – Trust in the Lord with all your heart, and do not rely on your own insight. In all your ways acknowledge him, and he will make straight your paths. Do not be wise in your own eyes; fear the Lord, and turn away from evil.

Proverbs 23:26 – My child, give me your heart, and let your eyes observe my ways.

Matthew 16:24–25 – "If any want to become my followers, let them deny themselves and take up their cross and follow me. For those who want to save their life will lose it, and those who lose their life for my sake will find it."

Romans 8:6–9 – To set the mind on the flesh is death, but to set the mind on the Spirit is life and peace. For this reason the mind that is set on the flesh is hostile to God; it does not submit to God's law – indeed it cannot, and those who are in the flesh cannot please God.

Ephesians 5:21 ESV – Be subject to one another out of reverence for Christ.

Philippians 2:6–7 – Though he was in the form of God, he did not regard equality with God as something to be exploited, but he emptied himself, taking the form of a slave, being born in human likeness.

1 Peter 5:6 – Humble yourselves therefore under the mighty hand of God, so that he may exalt you in due time.

What to Do

> Have confidence in God. God will provide. Trust Him.
> Be surrendered. I like the word "surrender" more than "submitted." It just seems more like a posture of faith.
> Submit as well. Give yourself over to God's control.

- Be like Jesus was in the Garden of Gethsemane: "Not my will, but yours be done."
- Humble yourself and God will exalt you.
- Consider: What is your agenda? Can you relinquish it for a larger purpose?
- Think about the ways grace abounds in your life.
- Don't fear the devil. Love the Son.
- Realize that not every test is a temptation.
- Endure!
- Reconsider the words that are life-giving truths in the preceding pages. What other life-giving truths can you think about?

A Prayer

Almighty God, You are my strength and my shield, a refuge in times of trial. Uphold me with Your righteous omnipotent hand and set my feet on the solid ground of my trust in You. Lead me in Your way, lead me away from temptations. Guide me by Your perfect wisdom and Your glorious Word. And give me grace to lead others to trust in You, for You are all we need. This I pray in Jesus's name. Amen.

A Poem

Even If I Stumble

Even if I stumble, even if I fall,
I believe I'll make it, that I can do it all.
A glorious sense of triumph inundates my mind.
Nothing is impossible, nothing hits me blind.

Nothing seems to limit me. Nothing holds me back.
Jesus has a hold on me, I have no sense of lack.
There's nothing that I cannot see, taking me off track
Jesus Christ has set me free, nothing can attack.

I feel so victorious, as if I have been crowned.
Deep within, I feel a pulse, conquests all around.
Not a worldly honor, nor favor, I'm just blessed
As if I was invited to enter heaven's rest.

It's like a peace has come to me
And I can be what I should be.

AMEN!

Printed in the United States
by Baker & Taylor Publisher Services